MW01035831

Must Christians Suffer?

Kenneth E. Hagin

Unless otherwise indicated, all Scripture quotations in this volume are from the *King James Version* of the Bible.

Fifth Printing 1990

ISBN 0-89276-404-X

In the U.S. write:
Kenneth Hagin Ministries
P.O. Box 50126
Tulsa, OK 74150-0126

In Canada write:
Kenneth Hagin Ministries
P.O. Box 335
Islington (Toronto), Ontario
Canada, M9A 4X3

BOOKS BY KENNETH E. HAGIN

*Redeemed From Poverty, Sickness and Spiritual Death
*What Faith Is
*Seven Vital Steps To Receiving the Holy Spirit
*Right and Wrong Thinking
 Prayer Secrets
*Authority of the Believer (foreign only)
*How To Turn Your Faith Loose
 The Key to Scriptural Healing
 Praying To Get Results
 The Present-Day Ministry of Jesus Christ
 The Gift of Prophecy
 Healing Belongs to Us
 The Real Faith
*The Interceding Christian
 How You Can Know the Will of God
 Man on Three Dimensions
 The Human Spirit
 Turning Hopeless Situations Around
 Casting Your Cares Upon the Lord
 Seven Steps for Judging Prophecy
 Faith Food for Autumn
 Faith Food for Winter
 Faith Food for Spring
 Faith Food for Summer
*The New Birth
*Why Tongues?
*In Him
*God's Medicine
*You Can Have What You Say
 How To Write Your Own Ticket With God
*Don't Blame God
*Words
 Plead Your Case
*How To Keep Your Healing
 Laying on of Hands
 A Better Covenant
 Having Faith in Your Faith
 Five Hindrances to Growth in Grace
 Why Do People Fall Under the Power?
 The Bible Way To Receive the Holy Spirit
 Godliness Is Profitable
 I Went to Hell
 Three Big Words
 Obedience in Finances
 His Name Shall Be Called Wonderful
 Paul's Revelation: The Gospel of Reconciliation
 How To Walk in Love
 The Precious Blood of Jesus
 Love Never Fails
 How God Taught Me About Prosperity
 Learning To Forget
 The Coming Restoration
 The Gifts and Calling of God
 Signs of the Times

Learning To Flow With the Spirit of God
The Glory of God
Hear and Be Healed
*New Thresholds of Faith
*Prevailing Prayer to Peace
Concerning Spiritual Gifts
Bible Faith Study Course
Bible Prayer Study Course
The Holy Spirit and His Gifts
*The Ministry Gifts (Study Guide)
Seven Things You Should Know About Divine Healing
El Shaddai
Zoe: The God-Kind of Life
A Commonsense Guide to Fasting
Must Christians Suffer?
The Woman Question
The Believer's Authority
Ministering to Your Family
How You Can Be Led by the Spirit of God
What To Do When Faith Seems Weak and Victory Lost
The Name of Jesus
Growing Up, Spiritually
Bodily Healing and the Atonement
Exceedingly Growing Faith
Understanding the Anointing
I Believe in Visions
Understanding How To Fight the Good Fight of Faith
The Art of Intercession
Plans, Purposes, and Pursuits

BOOKS BY KENNETH HAGIN JR.

*Man's Impossibility — God's Possibility
Because of Jesus
The Key to the Supernatural
*Faith Worketh by Love
Blueprint for Building Strong Faith
*Seven Hindrances to Healing
*The Past Tense of God's Word
Healing: A Forever-Settled Subject
How To Make the Dream God Gave You Come True
Faith Takes Back What the Devil's Stolen
"The Prison Door Is Open — What Are You Still Doing Inside?"
Itching Ears
Where Do We Go From Here?
How To Be a Success in Life
Get Acquainted With God
Showdown With the Devil
Unforgiveness
The Answer for Oppression
Is Your Miracle Passing You By?
Commanding Power
The Life of Obedience
Ministering to the Brokenhearted

*These titles are also available in Spanish. Information about other foreign translations of several of the above titles (i.e., Dutch, Finnish, French, German, Indonesian, Polish, Russian, Swahili, and Swedish) may be obtained by writing to: Kenneth Hagin Ministries, P.O. Box 50126, Tulsa, Oklahoma 74150-0126.

Contents

Chapter 1
Must Christians Suffer Sickness?

For as the heavens are higher than the earth, so are my ways higher than your ways, and my thoughts than your thoughts.

— Isaiah 55:9

One great lesson to be learned by the born-again Christian is that God has His own way of working out His will in our lives.

Here is a side of truth we don't necessarily like to hear. (Discussing Bible truths is like climbing a mountain. You climb up one side and have one view, but you climb up another side and have another view.) The Bible says, concerning Jesus, that He was perfected by the things He suffered. The Book of Hebrews tells us:

HEBREWS 5:8,9
8   Though he were a Son, yet learned he obedience by the things which he suffered;
9   And being made perfect, he became the author of eternal salvation unto all them that obey him.

When we get into this area of suffering, people get tangled up. They have done the same thing with suffering as they have done with the subject of prayer.

The Church as a whole has taken all prayer and put it in the same sack, shaken it up together, and poured it all out. But the Bible teaches that there are different kinds of prayer and one kind can't take the place of another. Every kind is important in its place.

The same thing is true concerning suffering. People have put it all in a sack and shaken it out together. They

1

have become confused.

Notice in First Peter 2:9-23:

> **1 PETER 2:9-23**
> **9** But ye are a chosen generation, a royal priesthood, an holy nation, a peculiar people; that ye should shew forth the praises of him who hath called you out of darkness into his marvellous light:
> **10** Which in time past were not a people, but are now the people of God: which had not obtained mercy, but now have obtained mercy.
> **11** Dearly beloved, I beseech you as strangers and pilgrims, abstain from fleshly lusts, which war against the soul;
> **12** Having your conversation [or, in the Greek, your manner of life, or conduct] honest among the Gentiles: that, whereas they speak against you as evildoers, they may by your good works, which they shall behold, glorify God in the day of visitation.
> **13** Submit yourselves to every ordinance of man for the Lord's sake: whether it be to the king, as supreme;
> **14** Or unto governors, as unto them that are sent by him for the punishment of evildoers, and for the praise of them that do well.
> **15** For so is the will of God, that with well doing ye may put to silence the ignorance of foolish men:
> **16** As free, and not using your liberty for a cloak of maliciousness, but as the servants of God.
> **17** Honour all men. Love the brotherhood. Fear God. Honour the king.
> **18** Servants, be subject to your masters with all fear; not only to the good and gentle, but also to the froward.
> **19** For this is thankworthy, if a man for conscience toward God endure grief, suffering wrongfully.

When the Bible talks about suffering, that doesn't mean "sickness." We have no business suffering sickness and disease, because Jesus redeemed us from that. A lot of times people who are sick say they are suffering for the Lord. No! They're not suffering for the Lord.

But the Bible does speak about enduring grief; suffering wrongfully.

> **20** For what glory is it, if, when ye be buffeted for your faults, ye shall take it patiently? but if, when ye do well, and suffer for it, ye take it patiently, this is acceptable with God.
> **21** For even hereunto were ye called: because Christ also suffered for us [now notice], leaving us an example, that ye should follow his steps:

Here's something you need to distinguish between: the example of Christ in suffering, and the substitution of Christ in suffering. We can follow His example in suffering, but not His substitution, because in that, He was taking our place. Notice the Bible says, *"leaving us an example, that ye should follow his steps."*

> **22** Who did no sin, neither was guile found in his mouth:
> **23** Who, when he was reviled, reviled not again; when he suffered, he threatened not; but committed himself to him that judgeth righteously.

In His being reviled, in His persecution, in His being spoken against, He suffered. But in suffering death, in shedding His blood, in taking our sins upon Himself, He was our Substitute.

He suffered so we won't have to. On the other hand, we do suffer persecution. People talk about you; they revile you. That's what the Scriptures are saying. When Jesus was reviled or threatened by people, He didn't threaten them. He went right on. In the same way, I just keep putting out the truth; I don't take time to answer critics.

Think about what Jesus suffered. Philippians 2:7 says, *"But made himself of no reputation, and took upon him the form of a servant, and was made in the likeness of men."* That was a terrible price to pay, wasn't it? Think what He had to suffer to do that. Another translation says, "He laid aside His mighty power and glory and became as mere men." And another reads, "He laid aside ALL of His rights, His privileges, and His rightful dignity, and was born a human being."

Think about what that cost. He learned obedience through suffering. He was already obedient to the cross. He didn't learn that; He was already obedient to come and do His Father's will. But He was made perfect through the things He suffered.

Hebrews 2:18 tells us Jesus suffered temptation. *"For in that he himself hath suffered being tempted, he is able to succour them that are tempted."* We suffer temptation, don't we? But, thank God, He is able to keep us. He is able to succor them that are tempted because He was tempted in all points like we are.

Hebrews 4:15 says, *"For we have not an high priest which cannot be touched with the feeling of our infirmities; but was in all points tempted like as we are, yet without sin."*

The 16th verse says:

HEBREWS 4:16
16 Let us therefore come boldly unto the throne of grace, that we may obtain mercy, and find grace to help in time of need.

Notice, in Hebrews again, *"Who can have compassion on the ignorant, and on them that are out of the way; for that he himself also is compassed with infirmity"* (Heb. 5:2).

These are the things He suffered. Thank God He can help us.

Let's look at the Acts of the Apostles to see what is said about suffering.

ACTS 5:41
41 And they departed from the presence of the council, rejoicing that they were counted worthy to suffer shame for his name.

That verse refers to the apostles who had been imprisoned and beaten for teaching in the Name of Jesus.

We don't suffer shame for the Name of Jesus in this country like people sometimes do in other countries — and like they did in the Early Church. But they rejoiced that they were counted worthy to suffer shame for His Name.

Let's look at the ninth chapter of Acts. This tells about the conversion of Saul of Tarsus.

ACTS 9:10-16
10 And there was a certain disciple at Damascus, named Ananias; and to him said the Lord in a vision, Ananias. And he said, Behold, I am here, Lord.
11 And the Lord said unto him, Arise, and go into the street which is called Straight, and enquire in the house of Judas for one called Saul of Tarsus: for, behold, he prayeth,
12 And hath seen in a vision a man named Ananias coming in, and putting his hand on him, that he might receive his sight.
13 Then Ananias answered, Lord, I have heard by many of this man, how much evil he hath done to thy saints at Jerusalem:
14 And here he hath authority from the chief priests to bind all that call on thy name.

15 But the Lord said unto him, Go thy way: for he is a chosen vessel unto me, to bear my name before the Gentiles, and kings, and the children of Israel:

Pay special attention to the sixteenth verse:

16 For I will shew him how great things he must suffer for my name's sake.

Jesus said that. Now, Paul didn't suffer sickness and disease. That's where people get mixed up. What did he suffer? We find the answer in Second Corinthians:

2 CORINTHIANS 6:4-6
4 But in all things approving ourselves as the ministers of God, in much patience, in afflictions, in necessities, in distresses,
5 In stripes, in imprisonments, in tumults, in labours, in watchings, in fastings;
6 By pureness, by knowledge, by longsuffering, by kindness, by the Holy Ghost, by love unfeigned.

We talk about people being afflicted with sickness. But the Greek word translated "affliction" means "in tests" or "in trials."
Let's look further at Second Corinthians 11:

2 CORINTHIANS 11:23-31
23 Are they ministers of Christ? (I speak as a fool) I am more; in labours more abundant, in stripes above measure, in prisons more frequent, in deaths oft.
24 Of the Jews five times received I forty stripes save one.
25 Thrice was I beaten with rods, once was I stoned, thrice I suffered shipwreck, a night and a day I have been in the deep;
26 In journeyings often . . . in perils by the heathen, in perils in the city, in perils in the wilderness, in perils in

the sea, in perils among false brethren; [That's about
the worst peril there is; it's difficult to suffer, too!]
**27 In weariness and painfulness, in watchings often,
in hunger and thirst, in fastings often, in cold and
nakedness.**
**28 Beside those things that are without, that which
cometh upon me daily, the care of all the churches.**
**29 Who is weak, and I am not weak? who is offended,
and I burn not?**
**30 If I must needs glory, I will glory of the things
which concern mine infirmities.** ["Infirmities" in that
case doesn't mean sickness. Infirmities are the tests and
trials he just got through talking about.]
**31 The God and Father of our Lord Jesus Christ,
which is blessed for evermore, knoweth that I lie not.**

That will give you some idea of the things Paul suffered. Let's look at another Scripture passage, Romans
8:17 and 18:

ROMANS 8:17,18
**17 And if children, then heirs; heirs of God, and joint-
heirs with Christ; if so be that we suffer with him, that
we may be also glorified together.**

Notice Paul is not talking about suffering in the sense
that Jesus suffered as our Substitute when He went to the
cross and died. (Now, a person might die as a martyr for
Christ in some countries.) Paul is not talking about suffering with sickness and disease either. He is talking about
persecution. Notice the next verse:

**18 For I reckon that the sufferings of this present time
are not worthy to be compared with the glory which
shall be revealed in us.**

It's difficult for us in this country to relate sometimes
to the sufferings that Christians go through in other coun-

tries. We have the freedom to worship God as we see fit.
But in other countries people receive much more persecution than we do here.

Let's look at more Scripture:

> **2 CORINTHIANS 1:3-11**
> **3 Blessed be God, even the Father of our Lord Jesus
> Christ, the Father of mercies, and the God of all com-
> fort;**
> **4 Who comforteth us in all our tribulation, that we
> may be able to comfort them which are in any trouble,
> by the comfort wherewith we ourselves are comforted
> of God.**

When Paul says "in all our tribulation," we could read
that "suffering." Is he talking about suffering with sickness and disease? No! He's talking about persecution.

> **5 For as the sufferings of Christ abound in us, so our
> consolation also aboundeth by Christ.**

Now again, Paul is not talking here about Christ being
made sin for us. He did that once and for all going to the
cross. Paul is talking about Christ being persecuted. Jesus
said to His disciples, *"If the world hate you, ye know that it
hated me before it hated you"* (John 15:18).

> **6 And whether we be afflicted, it is for your consola-
> tion and salvation, which is effectual in the enduring
> of the same sufferings which we also suffer: or
> whether we be comforted, it is for your consolation
> and salvation.**
> **7 And our hope of you is stedfast, knowing, that as
> ye are partakers of the sufferings, so shall ye be also of
> the consolation.**
> **8 For we would not, brethren, have you ignorant of
> our trouble which came to us in Asia, that we were**

pressed out of measure, above strength, insomuch
that we despaired even of life:
9 But we had the sentence of death in ourselves, that
we should not trust in ourselves, but in God which
raiseth the dead:
10 Who delivered us from so great a death, and doth
deliver: in whom we trust that he will yet deliver us;
11 Ye also helping together by prayer for us, that for
the gift bestowed upon us by the means of many per-
sons thanks may be given by many on our behalf.

Now are you beginning to get the picture? Notice in
Second Corinthians 4:8 and 9, suffering is mentioned
again.

2 CORINTHIANS 4:8,9
8 We are troubled on every side, yet not distressed;
we are perplexed, but not in despair;
9 Persecuted, but not forsaken; cast down, but not
destroyed.

We don't know much about the real persecution Paul is
talking about here. Somebody in the world can say a little
something about you and you're ready to give up. We wear
our feelings on our sleeve sometimes. People say, "Well,
they talked about me." What of it — they talked about
Jesus. So rejoice and be glad. Did you ever stop to think
that the Bible says, *"Yea, and all that will live godly in
Christ Jesus shall suffer persecution"* (2 Tim. 3:12)? Are
you suffering any persecution? If not, it may be because
you're not living right. If you can't suffer, be opposed, be
talked about, and be persecuted, you'd better quit now.
When you go out to preach the Gospel, you're not going to
please everybody.

Paul, you know, was beaten five times with forty
stripes, save one. That meant thirty-nine stripes, five

times. Three times he was beaten with rods. In Galatians
6:17 he says, *"From henceforth let no man trouble me: for I
bear in my body the marks of the Lord Jesus."* He bore the
scars of those whippings and beatings in his body. You
haven't been whipped or beaten yet, have you? You really
ought to rejoice.

In Colossians 1:24, Paul, speaking of himself, says,
*"Who now rejoice in my sufferings for you, and fill up that
which is behind of the afflictions of Christ in my flesh for
his body's sake, which is the church."* We have to interpret
that in the light of what Paul already said — what all he
had suffered. He did that for the sake of Christ's Body,
which is the Church.

Let's look at another Scripture. Second Timothy 2:12
says, *"If we suffer, we shall also reign with him: if we deny
him, he also will deny us."*

What kind of suffering is Paul talking about? Is he
talking about suffering with pneumonia, a bad cold, or the
flu? No! If we suffer like Paul suffered, we suffer persecution and all those things that go with it.

As I said before, we get by easily in the United States.
Think about the privileges we have. Whatever we give to
the Gospel or charity we can take off our income tax. Many
other nations cannot do that. Giving to the Gospel becomes
a greater burden for them. Sometimes they have to suffer
to build churches. But it is a joy — a rejoicing.

Many people think that when they learn how to believe
God they'll never have any more problems. A fellow came
to me after a morning meeting in Beaumont, Texas, one
time. He said, "I want you to pray for me." I said, "What
for?" He said, "I want you to pray that I'll never have any
more trouble with the devil." I said, "Do you want me to
pray that you'll die?" He said, "No!" I told him, "That's the

only way in the world that you are never going to have any more trouble with the devil." As long as you are in this world, dear friends, Satan is the god of this world.

God isn't bringing all this on you. He just said, *"For I will shew him how great things he must suffer for my name's sake"* (Acts 9:16). It is the devil who is going to oppose you.

First Peter 3:12-14 tells us:

> **1 PETER 3:12-14**
> **12 For the eyes of the Lord are over the righteous, and his ears are open unto their prayers: but the face of the Lord is against them that do evil.**
> **13 And who is he that will harm you, if ye be followers of that which is good?**
> **14 But and if ye suffer for righteousness' sake, happy are ye: and be not afraid of their terror, neither be troubled.**

And in First Peter 4:12-15 we read:

> **1 PETER 4:12-15**
> **12 Beloved, think it not strange concerning the fiery trial which is to try you, as though some strange thing happened unto you:**
> **13 But rejoice, inasmuch as ye are partakers of Christ's sufferings; that, when his glory shall be revealed, ye may be glad also with exceeding joy.**
> **14 If ye be reproached for the name of Christ, happy are ye; for the spirit of glory and of God resteth upon you: on their part he is evil spoken of, but on your part he is glorified.**
> **15 But let none of you suffer as a murderer, or as a thief, or as an evildoer, or as a busybody in other men's matters.**

Many people suffer as busybodies, but that's not suffering Christ's suffering.

A fellow in my church one time wanted to know, "What do you do with your money?" I said, "What do you do with your money?" He said, "That's none of your business." I said, "It's none of your business what I do with mine." It is no more your business what a preacher does with his money than it is his business what you do with yours. The important thing is to be sure you honor God first with tithes and offerings.

Now look at the 16th verse:

1 PETER 4:16
16 Yet if any man suffer as a Christian, let him not be ashamed; but let him glorify God on this behalf.

In First Peter 5:10 we read, *"But the God of all grace, who hath called us unto his eternal glory by Christ Jesus, after that ye have suffered a while, make you perfect, stablish, strengthen, settle you."*

Suffering will make you grow up spiritually in a hurry. It's the same in the natural realm. As a child your food and bed are provided — everything is furnished. But then it becomes time for you to get out on your own. You start paying rent, buying food, and making automobile payments. You find out right away whether you're mature or not.

As I look back now, I can see I wasn't conscious of the fact that the Holy Spirit led me into many hard places. Just knowing the Word and walking by faith won't mature you. That's the reason many people never get settled or matured — they won't stay in a hard place. I thank God now for all those hard places He led me through. I thank God for the nosey people I've had to deal with.

One time we were having a watch night service in one church I pastored. People would stay until after midnight and watch the New Year in. We didn't have any special speaker, and people were testifying about what different ones in the church meant to them.

I said, "I want to thank God for Sister So-and-so." Everybody looked at me, because Sister So-and-so was a gossip. She was a trouble-maker and was always sticking her nose in everybody else's business. She caused everybody, including me, more problems and trouble than anyone else in the church.

So I said, "I want to thank God for Sister So-and-so. She's been the greatest blessing to me of anybody in this church. She's kept me on my knees almost continually. I wouldn't have prayed nearly as much if it hadn't been for her."

Knowing her helped me! I suffered because of her, but it matured me.

Jesus, you remember, was *led* by the Spirit into the wilderness to be tempted. Luke 4:1 says, *"And Jesus being full of the Holy Ghost returned from Jordan, and was led by the Spirit into the wilderness."*

People want to accuse the devil of getting them in the wilderness. But Jesus was *led* by the Spirit into the wilderness to be tempted of the devil. The Spirit led Him. That's what the Bible means when it says, "He was perfected through the things He suffered." Whether you realize it or not, these are the things that are going to make us or break us.

Here's where faith comes in. And here's where the tragedy is.

People, listening to faith teachers, get the idea that they are going to sail through life and that everything is going to be "hunky-dory." They think they'll never have any trials, tests, or suffering of any kind. Then somebody rises up and says something about them and they're ready to quit.

You're going to have persecution. Jesus said in John 16:33, *"These things I have spoken unto you, that in me ye might have peace. In the world ye shall have tribulation: but be of good cheer; I have overcome the world."*

In the world you'll have tribulation, or persecution. The devil will put up every roadblock he can. He could hinder more in the country where Paul lived because they didn't have the freedom of religion that we have (or, are supposed to have).

You may find that God leads you to a city to build a church, and because you're Pentecostal — because you speak with tongues — people don't want you to build a church in that part of town. Perhaps they file a suit against you — I've seen them hold things up for years. If you know how to take authority over the situation you can bring it to a climax faster, but you're not going to escape having tribulation in this world. Satan is the god of this world and you've got to live in this world to a certain extent. He's going to put pressure on you. He'll try to keep that deal from going through.

People get this suffering business all mixed up. Someone gets double pneumonia and says, "I'm suffering for Jesus." That's not suffering for Jesus! Yet in some other areas, such as those listed in Mark 10, suffering is coming our way.

MARK 10:28-30
28 Then Peter began to say unto him, Lo, we have left all, and have followed thee.
29 And Jesus answered and said, Verily I say unto you, There is no man that hath left house, or brethren, or sisters, or father, or mother, or wife, or children, or

lands, for my sake, and the gospel's,
30 But he shall receive an hundredfold now in this
time, houses, and brethren, and sisters, and mothers,
and children, and lands, with persecutions; and in the
world to come eternal life.

We want to claim the houses and lands and blessings of
God, but did you ever hear anybody say, "I'm claiming the
persecutions in Mark 10"? No! We always claim the *land*.
And, we do need to claim the land to get it. But you don't
need to claim the persecutions — you'll get them anyhow.
Jesus said, "With prospering you'll get persecuted."

You've read about people griping because a preacher
had a nice house. What if he had a hundred homes? That
would be scriptural. I get enough persecution with just one
— I wouldn't want another! People will criticize you, and if
you haven't matured spiritually, that can throw you. To
tell you the truth, I'm immune to it. I've been criticized by
experts. I'm not going to let some little spurt bother me!

Chapter 2
Christians Who Suffer Unnecessarily

John 15:20 tells us, *"Remember the word that I said unto you, The servant is not greater than his lord. If they have persecuted me, they will persecute you; if they have kept my saying, they will keep yours also."*

Jesus is telling us here that we will suffer persecution in this world. But a lot of people suffer unnecessarily because of their own wrongdoing.

There was a lady, for instance, in my church back in 1939, who was very young in the Lord. One Sunday morning I was shaking hands with the people after the service and she said, "I can't do a thing in the world with my children. I've just turned them over to the Lord."

Her oldest children were teenagers, 14 and 15 years old. The younger ones, 8 and 9 years old, were always in church with her. But her older ones would be running up and down the streets during church.

I said to her, "Sister, you can't turn them over to the Lord." Now, I know after children grow up and leave home you can commit things to the Lord. But as long as they're under your jurisdiction, you're responsible for them.

I told this woman, "The Lord gave you your children and He told you what to do with them. You're not doing it. The Bible says, concerning children, *'. . . bring them up in the nurture and admonition of the Lord'* (Eph. 6:4). And also, *'Train up a child in the way he should go: and when he is old, he will not depart from it'* (Prov. 22:6)."

And I said, "I'm going to tell you the truth about the matter. If you don't get your children in Sunday School and church, your oldest boy will wind up in reform school and your 14-year-old girl will wind up with an illegitimate child." I don't know why I said that but it just popped out.

About a year after I told her that, these things happened. The boy wound up with a sentence in reform school and the girl wound up pregnant.

You certainly don't go tell someone, "I told you so," in a situation like that. The devil is already harassing them for their mistake. They're suffering — don't you think that won't bring suffering to a dear mother. But it was unnecessary. That wasn't suffering for Christ's sake. That was suffering for the sake of ignorance and stupidity. She didn't listen to the counsel of God.

Thank God, He's merciful, though. God was able to help that dear family. At the time all this happened, the husband was not saved. But he got saved, and the girl with the illegitimate baby got saved. She kept the baby and eventually married a young Spirit-filled Christian. They raised a family, and my wife and I visited with them years afterwards.

At that time they were faithful and on fire for the Lord. I remember that the mother said, "My son-in-law treated that illegitimate child like it was his own. You never could tell the difference." She told me, "If only I had listened to you, Brother Hagin. But I was just a baby Christian. I hardly had enough sense to get in out of the rain."

She told my wife and me that the boy had spent about six months in reform school. World War II began, and somehow he got into the service. "You're not supposed to get into the service with a criminal record," she said, "but somehow he got his record erased." He had eventually become a captain in the Air Force and had been in the service for many years. He and his family were saved and filled with the Holy Spirit, and were in church and on fire for God.

So that situation turned out well. If you'll believe God and trust Him, He can turn any situation around for His glory.

But the point I am making is that this woman suffered a lot. And yet that's not the kind of suffering the Bible is talking about. She was buffeted and suffered because of her faults and failures.

I think many times about the tears we shed. Ninety percent of the time they are selfish tears. Most of the tears shed at funerals are not for the person who went home to be with Jesus. Instead people are thinking about themselves: "Poor ol' me. What am I going to do?"

One time a very outstanding Full Gospel minister — in fact he was a district supervisor — went home to be with the Lord. He was quite a bit older than his wife, and she was grief-stricken. My wife and I went to see her and she was virtually hysterical. I sat her down on a couch and said, "Now, you've been in the ministry with him for a good many years." She was just a girl when they were married, and he was 30 some years of age. I said, "He's lived his life out and has gone home to be with Jesus." I began to read Scripture to her.

You see, the Bible says the Word and the Spirit agree. And the Holy Spirit will take Scripture and comfort you. I began to read, *"For I am in a strait betwixt two, having a desire to depart, and to be with Christ; which is far better,"* (Phil. 1:23). And I said, "Where has he gone?" She replied, "He's with Christ." I asked, "Well, what are you crying about?" She answered, "I don't know what I'm going to do." I said, "See, there you are, you're just thinking about yourself. If you had a son, and he phoned and said,

'Momma, the company I work for is promoting me, and I'm getting a hundred thousand dollars more each year,' wouldn't you be glad? You wouldn't start crying. You'd start rejoicing. He got an increase. Paul said, 'to die is gain.' " Before I got through talking, she was shouting. Her face lit up. She had forgotten about herself.

About that time some other ministers drove up. I get aggravated at ministers sometimes when they don't tell people what the Bible says. You could hear these men crying by the time they got out of the car. They came to meet this widow with, "What are we going to do now?" You'd almost think Jesus had died.

The pastors got her distraught and crying. I said, "You know, the Lord hasn't died. You all are talking about 'what are we going to do now?' You still have Jesus. You still have the Holy Spirit. He is going to put you over."

All the turmoil they went through was self-inflicted. About the time I'd get things straightened out, here would come another carload of preachers. If you could just get rid of the preachers sometimes, you'd have it made! You understand how I mean that, don't you? I'm talking about the ones who peddle doubt and unbelief.

Three different times I got this woman back into the Word, and each time she began shouting. My wife and I went on to my next meeting in another state. I would have liked to have stayed for the funeral, but my meeting had already been advertised. The day the meeting began, a day after that pastor's funeral, his widow called us long distance.

She said, "Brother Hagin, talk to me; say that again. The only comfort I ever got, I got from you. Everybody else pulls me down and tears me apart." I told her the Scripture again. She knew it was in the Bible, but she wanted to hear it again.

She said, "I could read it for myself, but it just helps to hear you say it." My wife and I talked to her long distance for about 45 minutes or an hour.

That was on a Tuesday, and on Thursday of that week she called again. She said, "Brother and Sister Hagin, could I just come over there and stay with you during the meeting?" We said, "Why sure, come on over." We ran that particular meeting three weeks. She came over on Friday, and stayed two more weeks with us.

She was so happy in the meetings — just smiling and enjoying the blessings of God. She said, "I'm going to be honest with you. Our own folks don't help you — they pull you down. They start crying and then I start crying. But I get around you and I start shouting. I'd rather shout than cry. I feel better shouting."

We told her we were glad to have her with us and finally she said, "I believe I'm strong enough now." She went back to her home state.

From that meeting we went on to another meeting, and then we went back home. She called us there and said, "Could I fly over to Texas and spend a few days with you? Back here everybody talks so negatively. I never did see it before. Everybody who sees me says, 'Oh, you poor thing. What are you going to do?' " We told her, "Sure, come on. We'd be glad to have you."

If we can't put something in folks, let's not take anything out of them. The devil is already working on that. So let's not join forces with him.

Some ministers of this woman's Full Gospel denomination heard she was with us and they wanted to come, too. By the time they got out of the car (and it had been four months since this man had gone to be with the Lord) you could hear them crying. Afterwards this woman told my wife, "I wish they hadn't come. They pull me right back down again."

We got her back up. But what I'm trying to say is that 90 percent of the tears we shed are selfish. This is true even among Christians. A lot of the suffering and grief folks go through is really the result of their own wrongdoing. I don't necessarily mean they've sinned. But just to think differently from what the Bible says is wrong. To walk in doubt and unbelief is wrong.

Chapter 3
Suffering in the Ministry

I've been preaching for years that God wants *all* of His children — not just some of us, but *all* of us — healthy and healed. God wants us to live our full length of time out here below without sickness and without disease. That's His best. Not everybody attains to it, but it's there anyway. You get criticized for preaching that.

For years I preached healing in Full Gospel churches and the very pastor I would be preaching for would criticize me. Pastors would tell me, "Healing is not so important." One fellow said, "Healing was just a side issue with Jesus and the apostles." And he was a Full Gospel pastor! I kept preaching healing every night. I hammered down that same line. His remarks didn't bother me. I let them run off me like water off a duck's back.

These are things, dear friends, that build character. I've had storms come in from every side. But the Lord would remind me, "The Spirit led me . . . ."

I went to preach a meeting for one fellow, and I don't know why in the world he asked me to preach. He knew what I preached. I had heard him get up right in the middle of conventions and criticize what I was preaching. Here he was asking me to come hold a meeting. I said, "Lord, I don't want to go." There's some suffering that goes along with that kind of thing. Don't think it's all joy unspeakable and full of glory.

I remember I started off preaching something we could all believe in. I didn't try to be controversial. The pastor said, "You preach on texts I never heard anybody preach on." That's just me. I don't try to be somebody else — I'm me. I never in my life preached on the prodigal son, for

23

instance. It's in the Bible, and that's fine, but I always preach on something else. Nearly everything I preached was controversial. I wasn't trying to be controversial, but it's just in me. It's the Word of God, and people didn't see that.

So I started out by going along with the people in order to get their attention. You have to be wise as a serpent and harmless as a dove. I got their attention, and then I began to drop a little faith on them. I just gave them a spoonful occasionally — people can choke to death on too much. When I would see they were slipping from me, I'd get back on some old Baptist sermons like "The Marriage Supper of the Lamb" and "The Second Coming of Jesus." I'd get them with me again, and then I'd drop a little more faith on them.

Finally I announced two or three nights ahead of time that I would be speaking on a certain subject. I had put it off as long as I could, but God had said, "Do it! Do it!"

I said, "Lord, why did You send me to this place to begin with?" I didn't know that you could hurt in so many places and still be in the will of God. But these are the things that will perfect you. They'll put some stamina in you. This is what it means to be led by the Spirit into the wilderness to be tempted of the devil; led by the Holy Spirit into a trial.

I remember something that happened when I was pastoring my last church. I was making plans to go to a fall Bible conference. I had preached on a Sunday night, and my wife and I were planning to leave for the conference the next Tuesday morning.

I stopped by my church office on Monday, and just as I started to go in, the Spirit of God said to me, "Fast the next few days. They're going to ask you to pray for the sick at the convention."

I stepped inside the church, and said, "Well, Lord, if they do, that's going to be more than they ever did before. They haven't even asked me to pray in the past. There are hundreds of preachers there."

My wife and I got to the conference on Tuesday and sat down in back because the building was full. In a little while it was time for the main speaker to begin, and the fellow who was introducing him said, "I saw Brother Hagin come in awhile ago. The Lord has been dealing with me the last day or two to have him minister to the sick tonight; to have a healing meeting." He added that another man would be the main speaker for the evening, and asked me if I would prefer to have the healing service before or after the sermon. The Scriptures say to prefer your brother before yourself, so I said I would go afterwards — and I made a mistake.

You talk about suffering! The speaker was upset because he thought I might ruin his sermon. He didn't like the idea of my having a healing service. He did choose a healing text — the woman with the issue of blood. And he did all right for awhile. He talked about miracles he'd seen in the early days of the Pentecostal movement.

But then he said, "I guess we shouldn't expect things like that in these times. Every movement is at its best in its beginning; then it starts to wane."

He began by getting people in faith, but wound up by getting them in the dark and in doubt, and then he turned the meeting over to me! There I was, having to wade through unbelief neck deep. It was like swimming in something — and I didn't even swim in those days! I could hardly keep my head above water. The atmosphere was charged with unbelief. God wasn't expected to do what He ought to do. All the ministers on the platform were breath-

26   *Must Christians Suffer?*

ing that hot breath of unbelief down my neck. You talk about tough! Thank God, I don't have to put up with that anymore. I wouldn't go through that again for $10 million. But on the other hand, I wouldn't take $20 million for it.

That's the thing that gave me stamina; the thing that perfected me. That was a kind of suffering. That's being led by the Spirit into the wilderness to be tempted of the devil.

Some of the biggest trials I ever had were the result of pastoring the churches I pastored. Some of the biggest tests a minister faces come from fulfilling the call of God upon his life. The devil will throw up every kind of roadblock possible. If you don't have the stamina and character to suffer persecution and trials, you'll not make it. You'll fall by the wayside.

I remember one time I was holding a series of meetings for a minister friend of mine. He and his brother, also a minister, were originally from a certain church in East Texas. I had arranged to go there and hold a meeting the following week. That particular church was looking for a pastor and they had congregational rule; they would vote in the man they wanted. I had told the deacon board I would come by and preach for them.

I was holding night meetings at my minister friend's church, and every afternoon he and his brother would come by the church and we'd pray. They would always ask me if I had prayed about that church in East Texas. I would say, "No! I haven't even thought about it, much less prayed about it. I just take one day at a time." The Scriptures say, "Sufficient unto the day is the evil thereof." And "Take therefore no thought for the morrow."

I said, "It won't hurt me to go by there and preach. I don't know whether it's in the will of God for me to take that church, and I'm not even interested in whether it's His will right now. I'm interested in this meeting we're having here." I don't get concerned about things like a lot of folks do.

On another afternoon we were praying in the church and the pastor got a call to go to the hospital to visit somebody. His brother went with him. I was walking up and down the aisles of the church, praying about the night meeting. I got to the back of the auditorium, stopped, and leaned on the end of a church pew. Very casually I said, "Lord, I guess maybe I ought to start thinking about that church in East Texas. I'm not concerned about it — whatever You want is all right with me."

The voice of the Lord came unto me saying, "You're the next pastor of that church, and that's the last church you'll ever pastor." His voice was so plain I almost turned around and said, "Who said that?"

I could have let the devil get hold of what the Lord had told me and thought, *I'm going to die!* Or, *I'll pastor there until I'm an old man — 103 — and then retire.* I didn't know what it meant and didn't take time to find out. I decided I would face what it meant when I got there.

About that time the two preachers came in and asked me, "Have you prayed about East Texas?" I said, "You fellows are looking at the next pastor of that church."

They said, "You don't know that church like we do. It's split right down the middle. Half want the pastor to stay and half want him to leave. He can't stay unless he gets a two-thirds vote, and he only has half of that. The half that wants him to stay is mad at the half that wants him to go. Half of them sit on one side of the church and half on the other. They can't get together on anything. You don't know that church like we do."

I said, "No, I don't know that church, but I do know
Jesus and the Holy Spirit. And the Lord told me, 'You're
the next pastor there.' "

That next week I took the whole family with me to that
town and we went to one of the deacon's houses. He said,
"Brother and Sister Hagin, we'd be glad to have you stay
with us the whole time you're here, but if you did, some
would think I was for you. They'd vote against you. You'd
better go somewhere else tomorrow night." So, we stayed
with another one of the board members the next night.
And he said, "Brother Hagin, I'm glad you can stay with
us, but some may think we're for you if you stay more than
one night. They might vote against you. You had better go
somewhere else."

We stayed different places and one night I whispered to
my wife, "You know what I'd do if I didn't know God was in
this? I'd get up in the middle of the night and we'd leave —
and wouldn't tell anybody we're going." But knowing that
God had led me there held me steady. I was perfected
through what I suffered.

We need to learn the way of the Spirit, dear friends.
And He doesn't always lead in a bed of roses or where the
going is good. He doesn't always lead where there's smooth
sailing and no opposition or persecution. But if you'll hold
steady, you'll come out on top.

Do you know why I'm so settled? It's because I suffered
awhile. You'll begin to praise God for trials and tests when
you learn about them. Each one is just another opportunity to prove God.

When I was preaching at that church in East Texas, we
stayed with a different member each night. A time or two
we even slept on the floor.

I started preaching there on a Wednesday night. You

talk about suffering through a service! Thank God for my
Baptist training. As a Baptist I had learned to preach from
an outline and I kept that outline right in front of me. It
was a good thing, too, or I'd have forgotten everything I
knew.

I went through that outline — one, two, three — and
every word I said came back and slapped me in the face. By
the time I got to the last point I felt like someone had been
beating me in the face. After some of these meetings my
wife said, "I feel like somebody has been beating me all
over with his fists."

You just have to suffer through some of these things.
Remember that Christ was made perfect through the
things He suffered. The Greek word translated "perfect"
also means "mature." Christ was made perfect or reached
maturity. Whether you like it or not, these are the things
that mature us. We need to learn the way of the Spirit.
He'll lead you into things like that. Jesus, full of the Holy
Ghost, was led by the Spirit into the wilderness to be
tempted or tested of the devil.

I had thought I would only have to preach at that
church in East Texas that one Wednesday night. But the
church board told me they wanted me to preach every
night through Sunday. They said, "After Sunday night
we'll have an election."

I knew the Lord had said, "You're going to pastor that
church." But I thought, *I wish He hadn't said that! I'd
leave!* I was so glad I had learned to preach from notes. I
could feel anointed and the minute I would step inside the
church door it was like somebody had poured a bucket of
cold water on me. Finally I said to my wife. "I'll go out
there and throw out a little dry hay, and we'll go home."
That was about all I could do.

We went on through Sunday night, and the deacon board said, "What do you think about it?" I said, "Well, go ahead and vote." I never did tell them God sent me. I didn't want them to know that the Lord led me into such a mess. I said, "The church has got to have its way about it."

They had their election and I got every vote but two. People said, "That's a miracle the board could ever get together on anybody."

So I started pastoring that church. You talk about a fellow suffering! I suffered for the first six months. I never did say anything in front of our two children. They thought everything was wonderful. But practically every Sunday night when I got in bed I'd whisper to my wife, "If I didn't know God was in this, you know what I'd do? I'd rent a U-Haul, back it up to the parsonage at four in the morning, load in our things, and leave. I wouldn't tell a soul. People would come by the parsonage the next day and find it empty. They'd say, 'I wonder where Hagin went?' They'd know the Rapture hadn't taken place because the furniture would be gone, too."

In the natural that's what I would have done. But I stayed and suffered. The Lord led me.

I preached the faith message when it wasn't popular. It's not too popular in some areas today. Yet I stayed with it.

I preached that God wants us to prosper. At that time I had only one pair of shoes and they had holes in them. I had a dime in one pocket and a hole in the other. The automobile I was driving had four bald tires and no spare. Finally the car wore out and I sold it for junk and lit out on foot. But I stayed with it.

One would not choose such a way to grow in grace. But God sees differently than we do.

What happens to many people when trials and tests come? They say, "I don't know what is going to happen to me. I've tried my best, God knows." But when they know the Word of God, they'll look the trials and tests in the face and say, "Glory to God! Hallelujah! Here's another opportunity to live by faith — to prove God. Here's another opportunity to prove the Bible is true."

Smith Wigglesworth said, "Great faith comes out of great tests." We read, *"Faith cometh by hearing, and hearing by the word of God"* (Rom. 10:17). Of course, you can believe what God's Word has promised you. But great faith doesn't come just by feeding on God's Word. Great faith doesn't come just by hearing cassette tapes. The *potential* of great faith comes by hearing. But the great faith itself comes when you put what you have heard into practice.

You see, faith is a force. To build up faith muscles, you have to use your faith against something. You don't build up muscles in your body just by reading books on building muscles, do you? No! It's when you put into practice what you read and start lifting weights that the muscles begin bulging out. Some folks have read all my books, but they don't have a muscle yet. They've listened to every tape. But if all their faith were dynamite, it wouldn't be enough to blow their noses! *You've got to put the force of faith against that test!*

That's the reason that after awhile, when you grow a little bit, you begin to thank God for the tests. Great faith comes out of great tests. Wigglesworth also said, "Great victories come out of great battles." I know Jesus potentially won the victory for us over the devil. But you've still got battles to fight, dear friends. There is no army that ever won a great victory without having a battle. There is no boxer who ever became a heavyweight champion of the world who didn't fight somebody; who didn't have a great battle.

When you learn that great victories come out of great battles, you can praise the Lord in the middle of the test. You already know the outcome — you know you are going to overcome. Overcoming faith belongs to us. It is ours.

We need to learn the way of the Spirit, because sometimes He'll lead you in ways your natural mind doesn't like. In pastoring for 12 years, I never did pastor a church I wanted to pastor.

I got the baptism of the Holy Spirit as a Baptist preacher. But then I received the left foot of fellowship from among the Baptists and came over among the Pentecostals. I held a meeting one time in a certain Pentecostal church and the Lord began to deal with me about pastoring it. It was in nearly as big a mess as the church I was already pastoring. And I was led by the Spirit into that.

The minister of that church wrote me a letter and said, "Brother Hagin, I'm leaving this church. The board asked me to write you and ask if you would consider pastoring this church. You preached here a whole month, so if you'll just consider taking it, they'll put your name up for a vote."

I wrote back and said, "Yes." I didn't say God had dealt with me already, but I said I would consider taking it.

I went there to pastor, and you wouldn't believe the mess I got into. You wouldn't believe all I suffered through. It hurt! But the Lord led me into the wilderness to be tempted of the devil.

At that time I was just 21 years old. The church had been there 23 years and some members had been baptized in the Holy Spirit for that length of time. In all those years they had never supported a pastor — he had to work for a living. I was the first pastor they ever supported. I learned later that this had been a troubled church — no one would have it. The Spirit of God had led me to take it, though.

I'll be honest with you — pastoring that first church in Pentecostal circles had more to do with my ministry today than anything else. I was perfected through the things I suffered.

When I would try to get an evangelist to come hold a meeting, no one would do it. I couldn't get anybody. Finally a friend of mine said, "Bless your heart, Brother Hagin, you don't know it, but I preached a three-week revival there and they gave me only a dime." A dime! Ten cents! That had spread among all the evangelists and they had said, "Don't go there. You'll lose your shirt and tie and everything!"

Finally I had to say to some of them, "I'll guarantee you so much." I didn't tell them I would take it out of my own pocket, if necessary.

I got some of them to come. (You can't blame them for hesitating.) We grew and God blessed us. When I left, more than 40 preachers put their names in for that church. They wanted it *then*. But they didn't want that mess before.

I was preaching a meeting in a Full Gospel church one time and the pastor invited me to stay for a missionary rally after my meetings were finished.

The missionary told how he had gone to a certain country. In seven years he had only helped two people receive Jesus as Lord. He came home discouraged, but God told him to go back. He went again, and in one year's time got 240,000 saved, and 70,000 baptized with the Holy Spirit. He started 50 churches. That's pretty good, isn't it!

All of his report was good, and then he showed pictures of some of his revivals. Finally he opened the meeting up for questions. One minister's wife said, "Brother, I notice you always tell something good. Other missionaries talk about persecution. Don't you ever get persecuted? Others talk about getting thrown in jail. Does that ever happen to you?"

I remember he looked up at me and grinned. He said, "I do like Brother Hagin does. Of course we suffer those things, but we don't magnify them. We tell about the good side."

I think that's what we do with the faith message. We tell about the good. But people don't realize some of these other things exist.

The missionary said, "I've had rotten eggs thrown right in my face while I was preaching. I've had over-ripe, rotten tomatoes thrown in my face. I've gotten arrested. We've been threatened with jail.

"There is a native worker who is a superintendent in my country. Because he and I are Christians, we don't bet. But we have a little something going. We have our suitcases packed, and we say, 'I'm going to get in jail for preaching the Gospel before you do.' "

Paul got put in jail. But where would he be if he had been griping and complaining? He'd still be in jail. Yet because he was full of faith, he and Silas began to sing praises to God at midnight. They got out. Paul was never sick, but he did suffer persecution.

We need to preach both sides, but we must remember there is victory in Jesus! It is well to remember that some of our hardest tests are God's way of leading us into a deeper place in Him.

That first church I pastored was a problem! I learned later that every church I pastored was a troubled church. I said to the Lord one day, "Why do You always lead me to those places?" I think He knew I could take it. And He knew I needed the experience.

My ministry wouldn't be what it is today if I hadn't pastored that first church. And it wouldn't be what it is if I hadn't pastored my last church. Some of the hardest tests I've gone through in 50 years of experience are because I was led by the Spirit of God. He knew the test was coming. It was God's way of teaching me.

You can't learn some things just by reading the written Word. It's when you put the Word into practice that it becomes real to you.

You can sit around all day and holler, "My God shall supply all my needs," and starve to death while you are hollering it. I've seen people holler all day long, "He took my infirmities and bare my sicknesses." Thank God He did. But when you put the Word into practice and enjoy the results of it, then you know what you are talking about.

Chapter 4
Suffering Because of God's Call

Some folks have it mighty easy in this day and time. But I feel sorry for folks who have always had it easy.

You know, it was hard for me to go out on the field. Our home had been like heaven on earth for 10 years, and here I had to be gone 90 percent of the time. That's something to suffer through!

My wife raised the children. She is to be commended. I get the credit for it, but she did it. She's the one who instilled the right principles.

When I went out on the field, Ken was in the third grade and Pat was in the second grade. I wasn't with them all those years. Then when they became teenagers, I wasn't with them. I had always looked forward with great anticipation to family life. The day after Ken was born I asked Oretha, "When will he get old enough for me to carry him with me?"

It's tough to be out on the field by yourself, shut up in a hotel room staring at the four walls. But God said, "Do it!"

When Ken got to be about 12 years old I would take him with me sometimes. I remember once we were driving back to Texas after a service in Oklahoma. We got home, and that night we were kneeling by the bed to pray. Ken began to cry and asked me, "Daddy, why do you have to be gone all the time? Why can't you be home like other daddies?" That's tough to take!

I tried not to be gone. I stayed out on the field for seven months. Finally I said, "It's too rough. It's too big a price to pay. I won't pay it. I'll go back to pastoring. I'll be with my family."

I cancelled my meetings. Cancelled my meetings!

On Sunday, July 10, 1949, I was planning to preach at
a church in East Texas. It was one of the best churches in
the area. I had been assured I could have it if I wanted it.

My wife and I went there that day, and I attended a
men's Bible class before the service. I was sitting on a
bench and suddenly my heart stopped and I pitched over
on the floor on my face. I fell right at the pastor's feet.

He picked me up and my heart began to race. You
couldn't detect the beating. It felt like something shaking
— like a bowl full of gelatin.

Some people carried me over to the parsonage next
door. I said, "Feel my heart." They felt it and began to cry.
Two more preachers came over. They told me later, "We
knew you were dead." I was cold all over and white as a
sheet. Death was upon my brow.

The ministers ran to the Sunday School addition and
one of them motioned to my wife. She was already getting
up. She told them, "The Lord spoke to me and told me
something had happened to him."

She rushed in and fell down beside the bed.

She said, "I feel like this is my fault! I was complaining
to God because you were gone all the time. And I heard a
voice speak while I was washing the dishes. It said, 'I could
take him where he would never come back.' I looked all
through the house — under the bed and behind the door in
the bathroom. I couldn't find anybody. I checked the doors
and they were locked. I just decided I was hearing things."

Kneeling there by my bed she prayed, "Lord, that was
You who spoke to me in an audible voice. I'll never com-
plain anymore. I don't care how long he's gone or where he
goes. I've made my consecration. I'll do what You said to
do, Lord."

The power of God fell on us. The power of God fell on

me. And I was instantly healed! I leaped off that bed and danced through the house.

Now, you remember I'd cancelled all my meetings. I didn't have a meeting left, yet I had a wife and two children to support and rent and utilities to pay.

You may ask, "Why didn't you just take a job?" I did do that at first. But I never lost sight of the fact that I was in the ministry and was living by faith. So I'd take any meeting, wherever the door opened. We had some of the most miraculous things happen.

I feel sorry for folks who have never had such a privilege. Some of you are driving Cadillacs and living big, and you think you are living by faith. You are no more living by faith than I'm an astronaut. You talk about the faith life while drinking malted milks and eating T-bone steaks! Now, you may get there after awhile. Don't misunderstand me.

But we had the biggest time. I think that was one of the sweetest times of our lives. And it was a time of spiritual growth.

We lived from week to week and hardly knew where our next meal was coming from. But we were never in lack, because our confidence and faith were in the Lord.

Learn the way of the Spirit. When I went out on the field I fought more devils in that first seven months than I had in the previous 15 years of ministry put together. If the devil could have kept me out of that field ministry, he could have kept me out of where we are now. I'd have given up on it. But I learned through what I suffered.

We don't like to hear that side of it too much. But when the Lord has told you something, stay hooked. Go right on through the tests and trials and be perfected.

Although we may not suffer physical persecution in

this land the way Paul suffered, some of our brethren in other countries may have to undergo some of those same things he did. And some of you are called to foreign fields. You are going to have to suffer some things, too. You may not have all the modern conveniences. You may be in an area where there is no electricity or running water. Don't tell me that's easy. But if God calls you, there will be joy in it. The Lord will bless you.

When I went out on the field, I told Ken, "Here's why I have to be gone. Your Mother and I have made a dedication to the Lord. God said to go. He'll make it up to us."

Mark 10:29 and 30 says:

> **MARK 10:29,30**
> **29 And Jesus answered and said, Verily I say unto you, There is no man that hath left house, or brethren, or sisters, or father, or mother, or wife, or children, or lands, for my sake, and the gospel's,**
> **30 But he shall receive an hundredfold now in this time, houses, and brethren, and sisters, and mothers, and children, and lands, with persecutions; and in the world to come eternal life.**

God certainly did make it up to us. I was preaching years later at a Full Gospel church in Cushing, Oklahoma. Suddenly in the night I sat bolt upright in bed. I knew immediately that Ken's life was in danger. He was in the armed forces at that time, serving in Taiwan. That night he had been riding a motorcycle and the front wheel had gone off a mountain. It was thousands of feet to the bottom. If he had gone over the cliff, he would have been killed.

When I sat up in bed, the Lord said to me, "You obeyed Me. If you hadn't, he would never have come back from Taiwan. But you obeyed Me. He'll be back. You can lie down and sleep."

So God made it up to me. Yet I had suffered during those years of field ministry. Many times when I left I would be weeping by the time I drove the car around the corner. I would weep all the way to my next meeting. I'd rather have been at home. There's a price to pay, dear friends. But, glory to God, we'll not magnify the suffering. I like to be around when payday comes! It wasn't easy back then. Some people want to start out where I am today. In some ways you can, and in some ways you can't. But after you have suffered a little while, and been faithful, it will pay off.

I've never shared some of these things before. I've said, "I'm a faith person — my faith saw me through." But the Lord began to talk to me about preaching this part, too. We've got to tell the other side.

It takes faith to go through these trials. Many times, after meetings at night, I would get so lonely. You are by yourself so much. I've actually thought about getting up and kicking out the windowpanes for a little excitement!

If you think that's not suffering, go through it and you'll find out. Yes, there is suffering, but not sickness and disease. Thank God you don't have to suffer with that, because Jesus bore our infirmities.

Say this: "I will serve Him. I will do His bidding. I'll do His will no matter what the cost may be." It costs something to separate yourself unto the ministry that God has called you to.

The foundation for my ministry today came in my staying put. I stayed in places where I didn't want to stay. That's where I learned so much. That's when the foundation was established in me.

Stay put in hard places, and you will eventually rest upon the mountaintop.